Who Will Dan Pick?

Who Will Look Out for DANNY?

CONTENTS

HAPTER 1

Abby lunged forward, her shoulders tense. Was Danny going to run into the water? There was a dangerous current at this beach, and he'd be caught before he knew it. She'd warned him, but he always forgot.

Suddenly, he stopped, flopped down onto his knees, and began to scratch the letters D-*a-n-y* in the damp sand. Then he stood up and waved to his sister.

"Look!" he shouted, delighted with his effort. Abby nodded encouragement, although at seven, he should have been able to spell his own name better than that. She'd spent enough time showing him how.

Still annoyed at the scare Danny had given her, Abby glared down at the notebook on her knee and scored angry lines through the words she'd just written. "What a ridiculous title for a story," she raged, "'Plant Life of the Seashore'!" But she could still see the stupid words behind the scribble. Trust old Mrs James from the Conservation Society, thought Abby. Only *she'd* come up with a boring title like this one for the story competition.

Who wanted to write about plants? They weren't exciting at all. Abby had written some really great stories about animals. Why didn't they choose something like that as the topic? She gripped her pen so tightly her fingers turned white.

Abby was small for thirteen. Delicate bones showed in her hands and wrists, and straight hair hung around her thin face. Anyone seeing her for the first time might think she was much younger, until they looked at her eyes. Then they'd be confused by the sadness there, and wonder what could have happened to make her feel like that.

Abby shaded her eyes as she sat on the sand-dune above the beach and watched her little brother. He grabbed a stick from the high-tide mark, and ran along the sand, dragging the stick behind him. His skinny legs raced out of control, and his unbuttoned shirt flapped like a flag in the wind.

Abby sighed, and wrote the title of the story for the second time. Then she drew a squiggly box around each word. "Plant Life," she groaned, staring at the sand-dunes that extended in both directions as far as she could see. "The only plant life here is the rushes!"

Last year, she'd won the intermediate writers' competition with a story about pigeons. She'd beaten Vicky Raymond, and won a book of bird poems. Winning was great! Then Abby cringed, remembering how she'd strutted around school, showing the prize to everyone, especially Vicky's friends. And now, this year, when they were all starting secondary school, and the first prize was a computer, Vicky would probably win the competition. And she didn't even need a computer!

"I'm the one who needs a computer," Abby muttered. She doodled little squares along the bottom of the page, imagining her fingers tapping out her latest story on a new keyboard. Abruptly, she jabbed her pen into the middle of the page. It wasn't just the stupid title. It was Danny as well. Looking after him every day made writing impossible!

"I'm wasting my time dreaming about winning," she muttered. Abby took the entry form from the back of her notebook and read the rules for the hundredth time. She stopped at the part she'd marked with a highlighter.

"Entries must be typed, double spaced, and on one side of the paper only."

Even if she wrote the best story in the world, that rule made winning impossible. Where was she going to find a typewriter in a dump like this? She wished they could have just stayed in the city.

At first, when Dad said he could get a job picking oranges for three months over the summer, it had seemed like a good idea. "The orchard is on the coast, and there's a beach," he'd said. "It would mean you three would miss a bit of school, though. Do you mind?"

Abby did mind, but Dad had already been unemployed for more than a year, and she knew how eager he was to work at something. Anything. It didn't matter what.

Her brothers thought it was a great idea. Seven-year-old Danny struggled at school. And, at sixteen, Leo had become more interested in sport and girls. When he heard there was a beach, all he could talk about was how much his surfing would improve.

Then, as she thought about it more, Abby decided it might not be too bad. She imagined herself reclining on a sunny beach, writing fabulous prize-winning stories. And there'd be no need to worry about maths and science for the first two months of the summer term!

But it didn't work out like that, not even for Leo. The beach was rough, and wasn't safe for swimming or surfing. And the only girl around was fourteen-year-old Shelly Clarke, the orchard owners' daughter.

After two days of boredom, Leo got a job in the packing shed. He didn't like the work much, but he enjoyed the money.

Abby had no time for writing because she had to watch Danny. He kept wandering off after butterflies or birds or anything else that caught his eye. Then today, when he was being reasonably well-behaved, all her ideas escaped before she could get them down on paper.

"And even if I do finish something," she grumbled, "I won't be able to type it until I get back to town. The competition will have closed by then. So why am I bothering?"

Abby sifted sand through her fingers as she wondered about the new school she would be starting next term. What would it be like? Abby and her dad had met her new teacher, and she'd seemed nice. She'd asked Abby if she had any hobbies, and had been pleased to hear about the stories and poems she'd written. "We have a writers club," she'd said. "You'll be able to join, and then use their computer."

"But not for another two months," Abby repeated as she chewed the end of her pen and looked down at her watch. It was nearly five o'clock, and she'd written nothing. They'd have to go back soon. Leo would finish his shift in the packing shed by five-thirty, and Dad would be back from picking. They'd both be hungry.

She snapped the notebook shut and tucked it and the pen into her back pocket. Then she stood up and flicked the sand off her jeans. "Come on, Danny," she shouted.

"Now?" His complaining voice floated up towards her.

"Yes. Right now." Danny could go on arguing all day, so she turned around and started to slowly trudge up the hill, a bundle of sneakers swinging from one hand, and her bare feet sinking into the soft sand.

Abby was sitting down at the end of the path tying her shoelaces when Danny finally caught up with her. He was dark and thin like his sister, but he didn't have her worried frown. Instead, his face was bright with the excitement of an entire afternoon spent treasure hunting on the beach. His pockets were stuffed with shells, rocks, and feathers.

Abby tossed his sneakers to him. "Here," she said, "put these on."

"I'm going barefoot," he protested.

"Put them on," she insisted. "Remember, there's broken glass further up the road."

"Oh," he sighed. But he sat down beside her. When he'd pulled on both shoes, he pointed his feet towards Abby. "Can you do up my laces, please, Abby?" he asked.

"It's time you learned to do it yourself," she said to him as she quickly tied his laces. Then she pulled him to his feet, and strode off up the hill.

"I'm nearly as big as you, Abby," Danny boasted as he pranced along beside her.

He's right, she thought. Glancing sideways at him, she was reminded of an ungainly young animal, such as a foal or a fawn, that wasn't yet in control of its legs. And she felt the same surge of affection that always swamped her whenever she was close to him. Some people said that Danny was slow, and this made Abby feel even more protective. When she turned to look at him, their eyes, hers grey and his brown, were almost level. He was going to be as tall as their brother, Leo, but not as solid. He's skinny, just like me, she thought.

Then she hurried him along, remembering that she hadn't bought anything to cook for dinner yet.

At the top of the hill, Danny stopped. Abby tried walking on without him, but she had to go back.

"That Danny!" she muttered in frustration.

The child's arms hung limp, and his head tilted back to watch three monarch butterflies spiralling around each other in the warm afternoon air. One fluttered off across the road and drifted down onto a swan plant. Danny followed it and squatted in the roadside dust.

"Come and see the butterfly," he called to Abby. She had to go back. There was no way to hurry him when he was tracking one of his creepy-crawlies.

The big orange-and-black butterfly spread its wings, raising and lowering them three or four times, then it closed them like the pages of a book, hiding the bright colours.

"Come on," Abby said impatiently.

"In a minute," whispered Danny. The monarch crept along the stem on spindly legs. It passed the swan shaped seed pods and paused on a cluster of narrow leaves.

"It might lay its eggs there," Danny breathed.

"We're not waiting to find out." Abby's sharp elbows stuck out as she stood over him, her hands on her hips.

"Well, then I'm coming back tomorrow to have another look," Danny persisted.

"You'll forget which plant," said Abby as she looked along the row of swan plants.

"I'll mark it." Danny kept his eyes on the butterfly. Reaching one hand behind him, he said, "May I have a piece of paper, please?"

Only Danny could get Abby to hand over a piece of her precious paper. Although she often sounded impatient, she couldn't refuse him anything, and he knew it. She tore out the page she'd been writing on, telling herself it was no good anyway. Danny grabbed the paper in one hand, then groped around till he found a stone heavy enough to hold it down. He tucked "Plant Life of the Seashore" among the stems, and pressed the stone on top.

"That'll do it," he said.

He can't organize himself to get dressed, or remember his homework, Abby thought crossly, but anything to do with butterflies is never too much trouble.

He stood up and took Abby's hand. He walked alongside her more quietly now, but she could see he was reluctant to leave the plant with its precious cargo.

When they reached the top of the hill, Danny let go of Abby's hand and turned for one final look. Abby walked on down towards the orchard, leaving her day-dreaming brother to catch up.

CHAPTER 2

From the top of the hill, the whole valley was a patchwork of orange trees planted in rectangles and squares, each block framed with a pale line of shelter trees.

To Abby's left were the packing sheds. Leo worked in one of them. At sixteen, he was one of the youngest workers. Most of the other packers were at least seventeen. Leo looked that old, though. He was tall and strong, with thick dark hair and a confident smile. It's just as well Leo's working, thought Abby. He liked to spend money, and there never seemed to be enough.

She looked back. Danny had crouched down, and was poking under a rock on the roadside.

"What's he found now?" she muttered. He'd always been like that. On the way home from school each day, he was always stopping and staring at things.

A shadow of worry darkened her thoughts. What would happen when they went home again after the picking season was over? She'd be starting secondary school at the other end of town. There'd be no one to look out for Danny, no one in the playground to deal with Vicky's little brother, James – the bully! James was always teasing Danny about going to special reading lessons and needing someone to help him write.

And who would make sure Danny ate his lunch? Abby looked back at the boy's skinny arms as he prodded at something with a stick. He'd dump his sandwiches in the bin and eat only his fruit if no one was watching.

Then, remembering the time, she stopped worrying about what might happen next year. Right now was trouble enough! They were going to be home late – again. She marched back up the hill, grabbed her brother's arm, and hauled him to his feet. "Come on," she snapped. "Dad and Leo will be waiting."

"Now look what you did," Danny complained. A long, narrow creature, with dozens of legs down each side, wriggled off the end of Danny's stick and disappeared into the grass. Danny's eyes flooded. Tears spilled out over his dark lashes and onto his cheeks.

"Sorry," Abby said, feeling guilty. As she gave Danny a hug, a sense of hopelessness swept over her. No matter how hard she tried, she couldn't look after everyone the way Mum had. It wasn't just the cooking and the cleaning and things. They all shared those responsibilities. But now, four years after Mum had died, they still hadn't pulled themselves together.

Abby hugged Danny even tighter as she remembered the day that Dad came back alone from the hospital. His shoulders were hunched, and he was trembling when he told them Mum wasn't coming home any more. He couldn't say the word "dead", but Abby had known. She'd just stood there hugging Danny, who was a round-faced, little three-year-old. That day, it had been her cheeks that were wet with tears, and little Danny who had said to her, "Please don't cry, Abby. I'll look after you." No one had used the word "slow" about him then.

"Why, why, why?" Abby silently asked herself as she and Danny plodded down the hill, hand in hand. "Why my mum? It wasn't fair!"

"Hey, are you going to the shop?" It was Shelly Clarke.

Abby had been so deep in her misery, she hadn't heard the farm bike crunching down the gravel road behind them. It came from the big, old house where the Clarke family lived.

"Hop on. I'll give you a ride."

Abby was going to refuse. She liked Shelly, but didn't feel in the mood for her lively company at the moment. Then, before she could stop him, Danny pulled away from her, and flung himself onto the back of the trailer, overturning a box of spaghetti cans. "Danny!" she said. "Be careful."

"No harm done," insisted Shelly, laughing and leaning back from her seat to right the box.

If Shelly wanted a typewriter, or even a computer, she'd only have to ask, Abby told herself as she watched Shelly swing her long hair away from her face. A friendly smile and sparkling blue eyes completed the picture of a confident, attractive teenager. Abby felt a stab of jealousy as she climbed up beside Danny. Shelly was fourteen, but she looked sixteen.

There was no talking over the noise of the farm bike as it headed for the shop that sold supplies to the seasonal workers. To Abby's annoyance, they roared straight past the cottage where her family had lived for the last four weeks. Shelly hadn't even asked if they needed to stop before going on to the shop. She just drove straight to the building with the padlocked door and the hand-painted sign nailed above.

It's not even a real shop, thought Abby, who was used to the city supermarkets. It wasn't open all the time either, just when Shelly got around to it. She earned her spending money by running the shop during the picking season. It seemed to Abby that everyone had a paying job except for her!

Shelly leaped down and fished a key from her pocket. The padlock clicked, and she pushed the door open.

"You wait here," Abby told Danny, pointing to a spot outside the door. "I have to go back to the cottage for my purse."

Abby knew she wouldn't have much choice when it came to deciding what to buy for their evening meal. There wasn't much money left. It was always like that the day before pay-day. The orchard shop was expensive, too. When she'd complained to her dad about it, he'd told her it was because everything had to be transported from the city.

"It'd cost a lot more if we had to drive to town every time we wanted a loaf of bread," he'd said.

The only thing that was cheap was oranges. But who wanted to eat oranges after picking and packing them all day!

In the narrow bedroom where she and Danny slept, Abby stood in the light from the tiny window, and did a quick count of the coins in the bottom of her purse. They had enough bread, but they'd need more cereal for tomorrow's breakfast. It would have to be scrambled eggs, beans, and sausages for dinner tonight. Leo would make a fuss. He'd asked her to buy a can of peaches and some ice-cream.

"It's ages since we had dessert," he'd complained at lunch-time.

"If he wants dessert, he'll have to put in more money," Abby muttered as she hurried back to the shop. He could afford to. He wasted enough money on junk food!

Abby had already left Danny on his own for too long. She never could tell what he'd get up to when she wasn't watching. Once, when she'd taken him to the supermarket in town, he'd helped himself to jellybeans behind her back. He loved sweets.

As Abby walked back towards the shop, she knew she was right to feel anxious. Danny wasn't there. Maybe he's inside, she hoped, peering through the open doorway. It was dark in there compared with the brightness outside.

"There you are," she said, relieved to see him leaning on the counter. At the sound of Abby's voice, Danny turned around. He had a half-eaten ice-cream in one hand, and a chocolate bar in the other. The wrapper was peeled back, and he'd taken a bite. Both of the treats were new in the shop and very expensive. Now, after paying for the ice-cream and chocolate, she definitely wouldn't have enough money for the cereal, sausages, and eggs.

A wave of angry despair surged through her. "You can't have those!" she exclaimed.

Shelly's smile disappeared when Abby spoke, but Danny wasn't listening.

CHAPTER 3

In four strides, Abby had crossed the shop floor. Furious that Danny wasn't listening to her, she grabbed the ice-cream in one hand and the chocolate bar in the other.

"Hey," objected Shelly. "There's no need for that."

"You didn't have anything to buy those with!" Abby shouted at Danny. He knew about money, so he didn't have an excuse.

"But you do. In your purse." His voice quavered, and his eyes filled with tears, just as they always did when somebody was cross with him. It usually worked, and he'd end up getting his own way. But this time, she wasn't giving in.

"That money is supposed to be for our dinner, not for chocolate and ice-cream." Anger creased Abby's forehead, and her lips pressed into a tight line.

"I could have ice-cream for dinner," Danny said hopefully. He blinked, and his mouth flicked up in the beginning of a smile.

"What about Dad and Leo?" What are they going to have if you've spent all the money on ice-cream?"

"Hang on," Shelly interrupted. She'd been quiet until then. "I think ice-cream for dinner is a good idea." She smiled encouragingly at Danny. "It doesn't matter about the money. Let's say it's a present from me."

Abby knew she was being unfair, but the frustration that had dogged her all afternoon boiled over at Shelly. "It's none of your business," she raged, and flung the chocolate and ice-cream into the rubbish bin. Then she emptied her purse onto the counter.

"That should be enough to pay for it!" she snapped, grabbing Danny's hand and dragging him out the door. She didn't stay to see Shelly chasing the coins around the counter and onto the floor.

With her shoulders squared, and staring straight ahead, Abby marched past the packing shed. She hardly noticed Tony Bradfield, the young fork-lift driver, backing his machine in through the side door to park it in the corner for the night. She didn't see Jason, Tony's younger brother, staring at her as she charged past. Danny stumbled along behind her, rubbing at his tears with one grimy fist. Neither of them saw the green truck, stacked with crates for the next morning's picking, until it honked them out of the way.

It was having to stand there, waiting for the truck to pass, that cooled Abby's anger and let misery take over again. By the time she reached the cottage, her cheeks were wet with tears, and Danny was bellowing louder than ever.

"Hey, what's up?" Dad met them in the doorway. With an arm around each pair of quivering shoulders, he pulled them down onto the worn couch against the far wall. "Careful of the springs," he joked. "Now, tell me what's wrong." He was speaking to Abby. Her fingers clutched the empty purse, and she shook with sobbing. It wasn't unusual to see Danny crying. He used tears as a weapon to get his own way. But Abby? That was different.

"It's my fault," she sniffed, and rubbed her eyes with one hand. Dad held the other. Dust and tears left streaks across her cheeks. "I shouldn't have left him on his own."

She looked up at her father, and was surprised to see patches of grey in the dark hair above his ears. She'd never noticed them before. Grey meant old. Dad couldn't be getting old. Not yet! There were lines around his eyes, too. She knew he didn't sleep very well. Often in the night, she heard him moving around in the little kitchen.

Abby looked down at his hand, scarred from encounters with twigs. "We've got no money left," she told him, her finger tracing one of the scars.

"And Abby threw away my ice-cream," Danny said, looking up at Dad pleadingly, hoping for some sympathy.

Dad raised an eyebrow at Abby. "Did you?" he asked.

Abby nodded and told him what had happened at the shop.

"But you can't watch Danny all the time," Dad reminded her. "And he's old enough to know that what he did was wrong." He turned to Danny. "Aren't you?"

Danny pouted.

"Does that mean we get no dinner?" Leo asked, leaning in the doorway of the bedroom he shared with his father. He was barefoot, and his dark hair was wet from the shower. There was a frown on his usually good-humoured face.

"Yes. Unless you want to pay for it, Leo," Abby snapped.

"But I put money in at the beginning of the week," objected Leo.

"You still had plenty left last night," she answered back. She'd seen him with Tony and Jason. They were walking towards the beach, eating treats they had bought at the shop. She didn't get luxuries like that. Neither did Dad.

Leo blushed and heaved himself upright. "All right," he muttered, fishing a new leather wallet out of his pocket. "What do we need?"

Abby handed him the list.

"Can't you go instead? I've been working all..." he blushed and stopped. Straightening his shoulders, and combing his hair back with his fingers, he took the list and headed out the door. Danny stopped sulking and scuttled after him.

I know why he changed his mind about going to the shop, Abby decided. It's Shelly. He was hanging around there this morning, too.

Half an hour passed before Leo came back. "I got a can of fruit and some ice-cream as well," he announced, as he came in the door smiling.

"That's a bit extravagant for someone who's short of money, isn't it?" teased Dad.

"Shelly said... she said," Leo began to stammer, "it was on special." Dad and Abby both tried to hide their grins as Leo's blush ran up into his hair.

"Did you say Shelly is special?" asked Danny, slipping inside behind Leo. "I think she is, too." With dreamy eyes, he gazed out the window towards the shop.

"You're not the only one who thinks Shelly's special," Dad said to him, as Leo dumped the food on the table and escaped outside. A second later, he poked his head in through the window.

"How long before dinner?" he asked.

"Twenty minutes," Abby answered, clattering around the few pots in the cupboard.

"Right," he said, and disappeared again.

A month ago, when they'd first arrived at the orchard, Ben Clarke had shown them the little two-bedroom weatherboard cottage. Abby had thought it looked like a box dumped beside the orchard road. There was no fence and no garden. Long grass grew in clumps where there should have been a lawn. Paint peeled from the window-sills and the door.

"We don't have many families here," he'd said, apologizing. He'd swung the door open and stood there, short and stocky in his overalls, his thinning hair ruffled in the breeze that always came up in the evening, and his face reddened by the sun. He was the boss, but he worked as hard as anyone. "So, it's nothing wonderful. But you'll find it's better than sleeping in the bunk-house. You'll have your own kitchen and bathroom, too."

Mr Clarke was right. It was better than the bunk-house, but not much. The beds were hard, and they had to be careful with the hot water.

Only two elements worked on the electric stove, and the bottoms of the pots were wobbly.

Because Dad and Leo were both working all day, Abby had volunteered to do all of the cooking – not just take turns like they did at home. At first it was fun, like camping, but soon she began to miss her freedom. Abby also missed their big, roomy kitchen, and the vegetables that grew in their own garden. As she opened a can of beans, she thought sadly of their ripening tomatoes and the fat pea-pods on the vines at home.

Ice-cream and chocolate had taken the edge off Danny's appetite, so he wasn't keeping up his usual clamour for something to eat. Even when the meal was ready, she had to call him away from the trapdoor-spider's tunnel he'd found outside.

After dinner, Leo reluctantly helped with the dishes before disappearing again towards the shop. Dad spread out all of his drawing equipment – pens, rulers, a calculator, and paper – on the table, and opened a book full of sketches and notes.

He's wasting his time, thought Abby sadly. She sat on the couch with the box of books Miss Deane had given Danny to read while he was away from school.

But Dad would never give up. Even after being made redundant from the engineering firm where he'd worked for fifteen years, he refused to abandon his plans for the new hydraulic system he was inventing.

"They didn't want it," he'd said quietly, "but somebody else might, one day."

"Which book shall we read tonight, Danny?" Abby asked. Resentment dragged Danny's mouth down at the corners.

"I don't know. They're all really boring," he grumbled. "And they're too hard for me. I'd rather do some drawing with Dad."

Abby opened the first book. It was about a boy who played football.

"Danny will like this one," Miss Deane had said. "All the boys do."

But she was wrong. Danny didn't like the football story any better than the one about swimming, or the one about sleeping in a tent.

Abby's fidgeting fingers found a small piece of silver-and-purple paper on the couch. She crumpled it up and flicked it into the rubbish bin without really looking at it. She was getting impatient at Danny for being so stubborn about his reading.

Just then, Leo looked in the window. He beckoned to her. She was aware of the furtive look on his face, and his sly sideways glance at his father's head, bowed over the table. But glad of an excuse to abandon the reading, she pushed the books away and went outside.

CHAPTER 4

"What do you want?" Abby asked him.

"Shelly wants to talk to you," he said. He shuffled his feet, and his eyes flicked from side to side, never quite looking at her. Either he's nervous, or he's telling me a lie, Abby thought.

But there was no lie. Shelly appeared from around the corner, her blonde hair swinging as she walked.

"I wanted to apologize for giving Danny the ice-cream and chocolate," she said, smiling as usual and not looking one bit sorry. "It was just that I was eating when he came in, and he looked so mournful. I felt mean."

"He's good at that," said Abby. "It works with me, too, and I should know better. I shouldn't ever leave him anywhere near a shop on his own." A half-smile sneaked across her face in answer to Shelly's friendly grin.

"Anyway," said Shelly, "I can't take this." She held out the money Abby had emptied onto the counter. "That stuff was a present, really. I gave it to him."

Abby pulled back and her smile disappeared. "No," she said, putting both hands behind her back.

"All right, then," Shelly shrugged her shoulders. "How about coming to a barbecue at my house tonight?" She turned to Leo. "You, too," she said.

Leo nodded. "Great," he said.

"I can't," said Abby. "I've got to put Danny to bed. Besides, we've had dinner." A barbecue at the Clarkes' place could be embarrassing. She'd feel out of place. Anyway, she felt as if she was being set up.

"Don't be silly." Dad was leaning out the window. "I'll put Danny to bed. You looked after him all day."

"I'll have to get changed." Abby glanced down at the old jeans she was wearing.

"No, you won't," insisted Shelly. "I'm not." She was still wearing her boots and overalls. "It's not a party. I've got to cook dinner because Mum's away right now and Dad's still at work. A barbecue's the easiest thing I know, and I'm not even very good at that!" She grinned again, not caring who knew she couldn't cook.

"Go on," Dad said again, arching both of his eyebrows, and putting his head to one side, pretending to look stern.

It was nine o'clock before the steaks were fully burned to Shelly's satisfaction. Leo had already eaten three juicy sausages, appetizingly browned by Abby a couple of hours earlier. But he had no trouble at all consuming the plate of dried-up, scorched meat handed to him by Shelly. Abby wasn't surprised. Leo would eat just about anything. But she was surprised to find herself joining in, and happily crunching her way through her share. It was just so nice to have some company.

While Shelly had been dealing with the meat, Abby had raided the garden for some potatoes and the makings of a salad. Mr Clarke came out of the house in time to praise the vegetables and frown at the meat. Abby expected Shelly to be offended, but she only grinned and said, "You'll have to come for dinner more often, Abby." Then she added, "And Leo." Leo blushed. Mr Clarke looked up from his plate and stared at each of them before he continued eating.

"Bring your swimming things next time," Shelly went on. "We've got a dam in the river. Come on, I'll show you."

The irrigation dam was sheltered by overhanging willows. Nothing disturbed its mirror-like surface until Leo skimmed a flat stone from one side to the other. He was showing off. Then seven wild ducks swooped down out of the evening sky onto the water, each one leaving a pattern of ripples. Abby wished she had her notebook. All the words that ran through her head would be gone by the time she got home.

It was dark when they left, but bright moonlight showed them the way.

"I'll walk with you," Shelly offered. Just past the Clarkes' old house, with its wide verandas and attic windows, Abby saw a small building tucked away under an oak tree.

"That's my schoolroom," Shelly said. She'd noticed Abby's curious stare.

"But don't you go to a school?" Abby sounded surprised.

"The nearest school's over forty kilometres away, and there's no bus service or anything. Mum didn't want me to go to boarding-school, so I do my school work by correspondence," Shelly explained. "It's too late tonight, but come back tomorrow and I'll show you inside."

"I wouldn't like to work all on my own," Leo said, after Shelly had left them. "You'd have no friends. It wouldn't be any fun at all."

But Abby thought of all the books she could read, and all the stories she could write, if there were no interruptions. "I'd absolutely love it," she murmured.

That night, as Abby was gathering up clothes to be washed, more silver-and-purple paper dropped out of Danny's shirt pocket. "A chocolate-bar wrapper," she muttered, picking it up. But it wasn't the wrapper from the chocolate Shelly had given him when they were at the shop. That was blue. Where had this come from? Then she remembered. Danny had gone back to the shop with Leo before dinner. But Leo wouldn't have bought anything for him. Then it dawned on Abby, Danny's been taking things again! She looked across at the sleeping child. It would be no good asking him about it. He'd never tell her the truth.

The next morning at breakfast, Danny could hardly eat for talking about the swan plant with the butterfly eggs.

"It'll be covered with them," he told anyone who would listen. As soon as he finished breakfast, he ran off down the track towards the beach. He was all prepared, with a plastic bag and a pair of scissors in his backpack. Abby wanted him to wait until the dishes were done so she could go with him. But Dad said he could go by himself.

"He'll take ages, and we won't know what he's up to," she objected, thinking about what had happened last night.

"There's not much trouble he can get into down there," Dad reasoned. "And wouldn't you like some time to yourself?"

Abby was wrong thinking Danny would be away a long time. Dad had hardly gone out the door before Danny came back up the road. He held the bag full of swan-plant cuttings away from his body, taking care not to bump it.

Once inside, he lay the bag gently on the bench while he filled an empty peanut-butter jar with water. Then he carefully arranged the pieces of swan plant as though they were prize rose blooms.

"There," he said, standing back and admiring his work.

"Did you get the right one?" Abby asked, as she hung the last mug on its hook. "Had the butterfly laid her eggs?"

"Of course I got the right one," Danny said. "Look." He picked up a teaspoon and used it to lift a leaf. Underneath was a scattering of tiny, pale dots – monarch-butterfly eggs.

Danny was the boy who spilled his cereal, upset his cocoa, and tripped over completely flat areas of ground. Yet, he handled the swan-plant cuttings and the precious eggs so carefully. Abby had seen it happen before, but it always surprised her.

"So, how long will they take to hatch?" she asked him.

"I don't know," he said, his delighted smile fading. Then he asked, "What day is it today?"

"Friday. Why?"

"You could put it in your diary," he said. "You could write, 'On Friday, Danny got some swan-plant cuttings with monarch-butterfly eggs on them.'"

"My diary is for writing about things I do," said Abby. "You can buy a diary of your own." He could write about stealing chocolate, she thought to herself.

"But I haven't got any money." The usual tears flooded Danny's eyes.

Abby almost told him she'd buy him a diary, then she changed her mind. He had to start being responsible for himself some time, and anyway, there were plenty of things she would like to buy for herself.

"It's pay-day today," she said. "Buy a book instead of more ice-cream."

"But..." Danny began. Then he glanced at the jar with its swan-plant cuttings. "Yes," he said suddenly. "Yes, I will!" Then he disappeared outside, on the track of something else.

While Danny was outside looking for more trapdoor-spiders' tunnels in the dry earth beside the foundations of the cottage, Abby wrote in her diary. She wrote about the barbecue on the Clarkes' lawn, and she complained about the story competition. When she'd finished, she went through the entries for the last three weeks. She felt a little bit embarrassed to read her first few impressions of Shelly. "A show-off," she had written. She isn't really like that, Abby thought. It's more that she doesn't care if people know the truth about her – like she can't cook. Abby giggled as she thought of last night's charred steak.

When Dad and Leo came in at lunch-time, the first thing they did was give Abby the household money for the week. While they ate their sandwiches and drank their coffee, Dad said he was going into town after work to buy some more drawing-paper and another pen. "Anyone want to come?" he asked.

"Yes, please," Abby and Leo answered together. "Me, too," shouted Danny from the kitchen, where he'd been checking on his butterfly eggs. Sometimes, Abby wished they could go the extra two hundred kilometres home to the city for their shopping. But they'd come out here to save money, not to spend it on petrol. Anyway, it was fun to wander around the Friday night market, and on clear nights you could watch the yacht races from the beach.

Abby was wondering what she would spend her allowance on, when she heard Danny talking to Shelly outside the cottage.

"We're going to town after work," he was saying. "Want to come?"

"I haven't been invited," Shelly said.

She wouldn't want to go anywhere in our old car, Abby thought. She'd seen Shelly and her mother in a new, four-wheel drive jeep.

"I'm inviting you," Danny said. "And Leo wants you to come. He thinks you're special."

Abby looked out the window in time to see Shelly blush. For the first time, she was obviously stuck for an answer.

"Shelly can come with us, can't she, Abby?" Danny nagged when he saw his sister watching.

"Of course she can," agreed Abby. She was feeling guilty about the things she'd written earlier in her diary.

"Great!" said Shelly. "I'll ask Dad. He won't mind looking after the shop tonight." She bounced off up the road.

Imagine her wanting to come with us, thought Abby. Is she lonely?

CHAPTER 5

Danny sat in the back seat between Abby and Shelly. They played "I Spy". Abby was surprised to hear Danny making better guesses than he'd ever done before. He's trying harder because Shelly's here, she thought.

Leo sat in the front. He always did. There wasn't room for his long legs in the back seat.

"Do you kids want to come with me?" Dad asked, as he pulled into the car park.

"No thanks," answered Leo. "We'll meet you in the market."

"Where? And when?" demanded Dad, remembering other times he'd arranged to meet Leo.

"You choose," Leo replied, trying to sound mature and reasonable.

"By the foodstalls, at seven o'clock, OK? Make sure you're not late!"

"Of course not!" Leo led the way into the market. Shelly followed. Abby, with Danny in tow, trailed further behind. She didn't dare take her eyes off her little brother. She'd lost the other two completely by the time she and Danny came to the bookstall.

It took ages for Danny to choose the book he wanted for his butterfly diary. He bought a packet of six felt-tip pens as well, in spite of Abby's warning that he'd have no money all week for ice-cream.

"I don't care," he said. But Abby guessed he'd be scrounging off Shelly.

Keeping a firm hold of Danny's hand, Abby wandered in and out of the rows of stalls set up along the river bank. A light breeze puffed out the sails of the yachts crossing the sand bar and sailing into the estuary. They joined in the cheering for the yacht that passed the yellow buoy first. Abby felt a story coming on about boats on the river. "Stop it," she told herself. "A boat story won't win you a computer. Think about seashore plants." She dragged Danny away from the water.

They reached the foodstalls early. Abby was surprised to find Shelly and Leo already there. It must be Shelly's influence, Abby decided. Leo seldom got anywhere on time. While they waited, they sat at a plastic table in front of the Thai foodstall and watched a team of gymnasts from a local school. Leo smirked when Dad arrived panting and ten minutes late. But he was wise enough not to say anything.

It was when Dad went off to order some take-aways, that Tony and Jason Bradfield came up and began talking to Leo. It's easy to tell they're brothers, thought Abby, with their dark hair, pointed noses, and narrow lips. She watched the three of them drift off a little way. Leo was listening to Tony. He kept glancing towards Shelly, and then across to Dad, who stood at the foodstall with his back to them. Leo was shaking his head. Then Tony said something else, more forcefully this time. Jason wasn't saying anything at all, but after awhile, Abby saw his eyes flick across towards them. When she caught him staring, he turned red and looked the other way. Finally, Leo nodded. Tony slapped him on the back, and the brothers walked off.

"What did he want?" Abby asked.

"Nothing to do with you," Leo said.

"You might look older than sixteen," Abby muttered. "But it's a real shame you don't act like it!"

"What did you say?" Leo demanded.

"Nothing."

Shelly giggled.

Dad arrived back with the food before a full-scale argument could develop. They piled into the car and set off for home.

As they drove, they sang along to the stereo. They'd heard the songs so often even Danny knew them. Shelly joined in with the choruses. It was fun. Abby forgot about Leo and his friends, and their sly conversation, until she was in bed. By then, she was too sleepy to worry about it.

The next morning, Danny had his book and felt-tip pens spread out on the table even before they'd had breakfast. The jar holding the swan-plant cuttings was in front of him.

"Move them, or they'll get covered with food." Abby pointed to the book and pens. "And the jar should go back on the window-sill."

"But..." Danny began, until he saw Abby's determined frown. Slowly, he bundled up the book and the pens and put them on the couch.

Abby moved the jar. She decided to frown more often. It worked better than nagging.

"Can you help me, please?" Danny asked after the dishes were done, and Leo and Dad had gone to work. "I'll do the pictures, and you do the writing." He tumbled the pens out of their packet and picked up the green one.

Abby went off to make their beds while he began drawing.

When she came back, Danny had almost completed a picture of a boy bending over a swan plant. There was the outline of a butterfly above the boy's head. Danny was frowning at the six felt-tip pens on the table.

"I can't do it," he complained as Abby leaned over to look at his picture.

"Yes, you can," she argued. "It's beautiful!" Abby was astounded at the care he'd taken. She could see the spiky stalks and the bunches of leaves on the plant. The boy's shirt and shorts were just the right colour.

"But I haven't got any orange for the butterfly," he protested.

"I bet I have." It was Shelly at the window. She was driving the farm-bike home from the shop. "Bring your stuff up to the schoolroom. I've got plenty of colours."

Danny grabbed the book and the pens, leaving Abby to follow with the jar of swan-plant cuttings. They scrambled into the trailer, and bumped along with their legs dangling over the back.

Shelly parked the farm-bike in its open shed, and led the way into the kitchen. "I'm starving," she said. "I'm having breakfast before I get the pens. Do you want some?" She clicked four pieces of bread into the toaster and got out some juice.

Abby stared at the messy kitchen. It looked as if an army had eaten breakfast and no one had bothered to clean up. Automatically, she gathered the dirty plates and stacked them on the bench. There was no room in the sink. It was full of greasy pots.

"It's a pigsty, isn't it?" grinned Shelly. "But I didn't bring you here to clean up. Leave it alone. I'll do something about it when we run out of plates."

"Why don't you use the dishwasher?" Abby eyed the gleaming machine under the bench.

"It's full."

Of course, thought Abby. It would be. "Where's the detergent?" she demanded.

A few minutes later, to the sound of the purring machine, they sat down to toast and honey on the last of the clean plates. All the glasses were dirty, so they'd had to wash three before they could use them.

After breakfast, Shelly and Abby wandered over to the schoolroom, with Danny running on ahead. Abby was surprised to see that although the house had been left unlocked, Shelly needed a key to get into the schoolroom. "There's some expensive stuff in here," she said, pushing the door open.

The first thing Abby saw was a computer station against the far wall. It was complete with a colour monitor and a laser printer.

I had the idea she would only have to ask for a computer, thought Abby. Imagine having something like that, and not even having to share it!

"I wish we had enough money for a room like this," Abby said enviously.

"We don't really." Shelly sounded almost serious. "Dad took over the orchard only two years ago, and last year was a bad season. Grandad set all this up." She waved her hand around the room.

"You're lucky," said Abby.

"Dad keeps telling me that." Shelly's grin returned. "Anyway, Danny, can you find what you want in here?" She tipped a box full of felt-tip pens onto a long work table under the window. There must have been sixty or seventy of them!

"Just make sure you remember to put the caps on when you finish with the pens," Abby instructed him, dragging her hungry eyes away from the computer.

"He will," said Shelly.

"I wouldn't be too sure about that."

"If he doesn't, I won't let him use them again," Shelly said firmly. Danny's eyes rolled from side to side. He knows she really means it, Abby realized.

While Danny was finishing his picture, Abby examined the rest of the schoolroom. Shelves that ran from floor to ceiling were jammed full of books. Some of them were fiction, but there were also two shelves of "how to" books and magazines. Along the bottom were twenty volumes of an encyclopedia. One shelf had wildlife books about everything from insects to elephants. "Don't let Danny get his hands on those," Abby said. "You'll never get them back!"

"What?" demanded Danny, who had completed the butterfly, and returned the pens to their box.

"Did you put on the caps?" asked Shelly.

Danny nodded and held out the box for her to see.

"Good," she said. "Then you can see my book about butterflies." She lifted down a heavy volume with a brown cover lettered in gold. Danny carried it as though it were delicate china, and put it on the work table. He turned the pages with gentle fingers. Abby heard his excited breathing as he studied the pictures.

"Do you want to play some computer games?" Shelly asked. Abby knew she'd been seen drooling over the machine.

"That sounds like fun. Do you have any kind of word-processing programme?" she asked.

"Of course. That's what I'm really supposed to use it for."

"Lucky thing," sighed Abby.

"Don't tell me you want to be a writer!" exclaimed Shelly.

Abby shrugged. A blush spread across her pale cheeks.

"You can use it whenever you want," Shelly said generously.

"I don't know how," Abby blurted.

"I'll show you. Sit down."

Almost an hour later, Abby's shoulders ached, and her eyes hurt, but she knew how to use the computer.

"If only I had something decent to write," she complained. She told Shelly about the impossible story title the Conservation Society had chosen.

"Write my story. About the butterfly."

The girls turned around to see Danny leaning on the back of Shelly's chair. During their discussion, they'd forgotten about him.

"Good idea," said Shelly. "Go on and try it," she said to Abby.

It would be good practice, Abby decided. Then she glanced at her watch, ten past eleven. "Can we please come back later?" she asked. "I have to do something else first."

"Anytime," insisted Shelly.

"But what else do you have to do, Abby?" Danny pouted.

"Come on," she said, standing up. "You can help me." She pulled him out the door and waited while Shelly locked up the schoolroom.

Then she led the way back to the Clarkes' kitchen. Ignoring Shelly's objections, Abby began to unload the dishwasher. She handed the utensil basket to Danny and pointed him towards the drawer under the bench. "Put those away," she instructed.

"You didn't have to do that," protested Shelly when it was all done.

"I know," agreed Abby, "but someone had to." Without stopping, she cleared the table and benches, stacked the machine with the rest of the dirty dishes, and started it. Then she filled the sink with hot water and attacked the greasy pots.

"You make me feel very guilty," Shelly complained as she dried the last pot and put it away.

"Maybe you should feel guilty." It was Mr Clarke. "I've been standing here watching." He turned to Abby. "But what I don't understand is why you are doing the job Shelly is being paid her allowance to do."

"I owe her," replied Abby as she wiped the bench and rinsed out the dishcloth.

"What for?"

"For letting me use the computer in her schoolroom." Abby squeezed the water from the dishcloth and hung it over the tap. But she was also thinking about Danny and the chocolate he'd taken from the shop.

"That is all right, isn't it, Dad?"

For the first time, Abby saw Shelly look just a little bit anxious. Mr Clarke hesitated. Her dad's not quite the old softie he seems to be, Abby thought. Sudden disappointment hit her. Maybe he wasn't so keen about her having the run of all that expensive equipment.

Then he smiled. "I guess that'll be fine," he said. "You can go ahead and take the spare key. Just make sure you don't leave the door unlocked. And Shelly," he went on, "what are we having for lunch?"

"Not already!" she grumbled.

"I'll be back in about ten minutes," he said, pointing to the clock above the door. "And I'll be hungry!"

Shelly's face brightened. "Hey, Abby," she said. "How would you like to..."

"Sorry, not this time," interrupted Abby, laughing. "I've got to make lunch for Dad and Leo." She took Danny by the hand and led him out the door.

At two o'clock, Abby was back at the computer. She'd written: "A monarch butterfly laid its eggs on a swan plant. Danny found them."

"Come and look at this, Danny," she yelled through the open doorway.

Shelly was swinging Danny in a hammock that hung between two old oak trees. "Let's see what Abby wants," she said, and tipped him out onto the grass. Danny was still giggling when they got to the door.

"A monarch butterfly laid its eggs on a swan plant," Shelly read, pointing to each word.

"Danny found them," read Danny, pointing to the last three words.

Abby held her breath. Danny had read those words by himself. And nobody had made him! She'd never heard him read so well before.

"How do you know that says, 'Danny found them'?" she demanded.

"Well," he giggled, "that says 'Danny'." He pointed to his name.

"Yes. But what about the rest? How did you know that said 'found them'?"

"Well, I did find them, didn't I?" And he raced off outside.

"Why did you ask him that, Abby?" Shelly looked confused.

"Because Danny can't read. He's never been able to read."

When Abby and Danny went back to the cottage to get dinner ready, they left the jar of swan-plant cuttings in the schoolroom.

"I'm going to draw my pictures there, and it's too hard to carry the jar back and forth," Danny said.

"Sometimes you're pretty sensible, Danny," Abby told him. "But how do you feel about using Shelly's books and felt-tip pens after taking that chocolate from the shop last night?"

"She wouldn't mind," he answered, looking at her defiantly. "She would have given it to me if I'd asked."

"But you didn't ask. You just took it."

Danny's stare wavered. The corners of his mouth went down. He pulled away from her and raced ahead into the cottage.

Dad was in the shower when Leo came into the kitchen. Abby was spooning food onto their plates. If she'd looked up at him, instead of concentrating on what she was doing, she'd have seen the odd look in his eyes. Maybe then, all of the trouble might have been avoided. She'd have been ready for it.

CHAPTER 6

"There's a good movie on in town tonight." Leo dipped one finger into the gravy and licked it, then ducked back from the wooden spoon that Abby waved at him. "Do you want to come?"

"I don't have enough money," Abby replied.

"I'll pay," Leo answered quickly.

Abby put down her spoon and stared at him. "You'll pay for me? Why?" A puzzled frown wrinkled her forehead. This wasn't like her big brother.

Leo looked down at his bare feet and shuffled them on the cracked lino. "It's Shelly," he mumbled.

"What about Shelly?"

"She wants to go. But her father won't let her..." He looked up. "He might though, if you were going, too. I don't know why, but he thinks you're 'a very responsible young woman'."

An understanding grin wiped away Abby's frown. She couldn't see why Shelly would want to go to the movies with someone like Leo. But if that's what she wants, Abby thought, I'll do what I can to help.

"All right," she said. "I'll go."

"Great!" exclaimed Leo, and he bounded out the door like a Labrador puppy chasing a ball.

It was only when he came back a few minutes later, that Abby wondered how they were going to travel the forty kilometres into town. Dad would be watching Danny and getting on with his plans. He wouldn't be driving. Leo could drive, but he didn't have a licence yet.

"Who are we going with?" she asked as she carried the plates to the table.

"The Bradfields, Tony and Jason. You know them. We saw them at the market last night. Tony's got a licence."

"Is he allowed to drive his parents' car?" Abby had seen Mr Bradfield. He was the grumpy-looking supervisor in Leo's packing shed. She couldn't imagine him lending his car to anyone.

"Of course he is. He's even got one of his own, but it's got a flat battery. I'm the only one who isn't allowed to drive around here!"

"You will be when you get your licence," Dad announced as he came out of the bathroom, rubbing his hair dry.

"But I can drive now." Leo had his "you never let me do anything" look on his face. "No one would even know I didn't have a licence."

"I would. And driving without a licence is illegal. You know that," Dad insisted. Abby could see that was the end of the discussion. If Leo said much more, Dad would put his foot down about going to the movies.

They hurried through the dishes, and Abby went off to get changed. When she came out of her room, Leo was impatiently kicking a stone around on the road outside.

"Come on," he urged her. "We'll be late."

"I thought you said seven o'clock." Abby looked at her watch. "We've got at least another five minutes."

"But Shelly might be waiting. I don't want to be late."

They were the first to reach the fenced-off area where the workers parked their cars. The Bradfields turned up next, but they all had to wait ten minutes for Shelly. Abby's eyes widened when she saw her. Shelly's hair looked different to normal, and she was wearing make-up! She wore a black dress and carried a trendy leather backpack, and looked fantastic! Imagine dressing up like that just to go to the movies, thought Abby.

"Hi, everyone," said Shelly. "I hope I haven't kept you waiting."

"Told you," whispered Leo.

"Wow!" muttered Tony.

An uncomfortable shiver ran down Abby's back. Something wasn't quite right about Tony. She knew this for certain when he gave Leo a sly look, and said, "Let's go."

Leo nodded and took the keys to his dad's car out of his pocket. He looked uncomfortable as he said to Abby, "Tony couldn't get his father's car, after all."

"That's right." Tony swaggered around to the driver's door. "But you don't have to worry. I'm an excellent driver."

Abby felt bad about going. She watched the others pile into the car, Jason beside Tony, and Shelly and Leo in the back. Tony started the engine. "Get in," he ordered.

"Come on." Shelly's smiling face looked out at her from the shadows. There was no time to argue about whether it was right or not. Abby felt that she owed it to Shelly. She climbed in and pulled the door shut behind her. Tony revved the engine, and the car that had never spun its wheels before sprayed gravel into the air as it took off out the gate.

Apart from the reckless start, Tony's driving wasn't bad. He took the sharp bends at a sensible speed, and kept to his own side of the road. All the same, Abby felt too uptight to join in the laughing and joking. Did Leo know Tony had no car before they left the house? Of course he did. He must have sneaked the keys out of the jar on the bench. Dad would never have given them to him!

Leo had just wanted to show off, Abby decided, as she watched him look across the seat at Shelly. Shelly smiled up at him. Abby sat upright and stared straight ahead.

Abby tried to hide her nervousness. It was too late to make a fuss now. But she was relieved when they pulled into the public car park in the centre of town about an hour later. Tony locked the doors and put the keys into Shelly's backpack for safe keeping, then they all hurried across the street to the movie theatre. Abby began to relax a little as the film began. It was funny, and she enjoyed it. She started to feel edgy again only as they left the theatre and pushed through the crowd towards the car.

"Don't be silly," she told herself. "Tony got us here safely. He's a good driver. He'll get us home again." Then she wondered what she'd do when they did get home. Leo would expect her to keep quiet about taking the car. She didn't know if she could.

The crowd had thinned as they neared their car on the far side of the car park. The others stood by the car and waited for Shelly to find the keys in her backpack. Suddenly, a door opened in a building across from the car park. Music and lights flooded out.

"Sounds like they're having a good time," said Jason, who'd been quiet all evening.

"Let's see what's going on," suggested Tony.

"Come on," said Jason, staring at Abby. Then he followed his brother.

"Do you want to go?" Leo asked the girls.

"Yes," said Shelly.

"No," said Abby, at the same time.

"Oh, come on, Abby," Shelly said, grabbing her hand and pulling her towards the open door. "It'll be fun!"

"Dad will wonder where we are," Abby protested. "And we haven't got any money."

"Don't worry about money," Shelly begged, giving Abby's hand another tug. "I've got some, and we won't stay long, will we, Leo?"

"We can't go home yet, anyway," reasoned Leo. "Not without Tony and Jason."

Inside the building there was warmth and music and laughter. Tony had found a table, and was dragging chairs over to it. Jason was fighting his way through the crowd, his arms laden with cans of drink. Half the pickers from the orchard seemed to be there.

"I hope no one tells Dad that we were here," Shelly said, but she didn't look too worried. Abby didn't want anyone telling her dad, either!

The music was loud. Abby felt the beat like a deep thud, thud, thud inside her. Shelly tapped her feet and swung her shoulders to the music. Jason slid a can of drink across the table to each of the girls, but Shelly ignored hers. She leaped to her feet and grabbed Abby's hand. "Come on, let's dance!" she insisted.

Some of the older boys from Leo's packing shed came past as Shelly pulled her into the crowd. One of them nodded towards Abby, and she heard him say to Leo, "Couldn't you get a babysitter?" She didn't hear Leo's answer, but by this time she didn't care what they said. She was having a good time. They'd had lunch-time dances at school during the winter, and she was quite a good dancer.

The music stopped. They went back to their table and each opened a drink. Dancing was thirsty work!

When the music started again, Shelly got up with Leo.

"Want to dance?" Jason said to Abby. She nodded, and they jostled their way onto the floor. Neither of them talked much, but when the music stopped, Jason smiled at her as they walked back to their table. Abby decided he was a lot nicer than his brother. She was pleased that Tony had gone off somewhere, but no one else even noticed he was missing. They were all having so much fun.

The next hour passed quickly. Abby was surprised to hear the disc jockey say, "It's eleven-thirty, kids. This is the last dance." Eleven-thirty? They'd have to go. They should have been home ages ago!

Leo, Jason, Shelly, and Abby all looked carefully around the rapidly emptying room. Where was Tony? Abby waited anxiously while Jason hunted through the bathroom. No luck. They searched methodically among the groups standing around outside. There they found the boy who had made the smart remark about babysitters earlier.

"Yeah. He was with us about an hour ago. But he's gone now. Some friends of his came by, and he left with them. I don't know where they went," the boy said.

"What are we going to do now?" Jason demanded, looking at Leo. "Tony was the only one who could drive."

"We'll have to call Shelly's dad to come and get us," Abby said. "Where's the nearest pay phone?"

"No. Don't do that!" Shelly protested.

"Why not? Surely he won't mind?"

"He doesn't know..." She began to speak, but faltered. "I told him your dad was driving us. He'll go berserk if he finds out I was lying! We'll have to find another way home." She turned to Leo. "You told me you can drive," she said, and shoved the bunch of keys at him.

Abby watched Leo's fingers fiddle with the keys until he held just one, the ignition key. "But you haven't got a licence," she objected, grabbing his arm.

At the same time, Shelly was saying, "No one will know. There aren't any police around."

"All right," Leo said, shaking free of Abby's grasp. "Get in."

Shelly climbed into the front seat. Jason and a reluctant Abby got in the back. The car finally started on the third attempt. Leo had never driven at night, so it took him a minute to find the lights. He slowly reversed out of the park in a series of sharp jerks. Their car was the last to leave the car park, but Leo kept stopping and looking over his shoulder, as if he was afraid of backing into something. At last they were out of the town and heading towards the orchard.

Abby was relieved that Leo drove slowly. She was surprised, too, because when he was driving with Dad, he had to be told every few minutes to slow down. He must have been as nervous as she was.

They were almost there – only a few kilometres to go – when Leo turned left onto the narrow orchard road. A few seconds later, a light behind them began closing in on them quickly! It was a police officer on a motorcycle, with lights flashing and siren wailing.

"You forgot to signal," the police officer said to Leo as he looked in the window after they'd stopped. "Would you step out of the car and show me your licence please?"

Abby knew she'd never be able to forget the next ten minutes. The officer began by noting Leo's inability to produce a licence. Leo stammered out something about losing it. Abby could see the police officer didn't believe him. The nightmare went on and on, until a car, coming from the direction of the orchard, pulled up beside them. Two people got out. Their dark shapes were silhouetted in the lights of the cars.

"Is that you, Shelly?" a voice called. It was Mr Clarke. Poor Shelly, she's caught, thought Abby. Then she realized the truth – they were all caught!

"Leo!" Abby heard her father call. "Do you know where Abby is?"

"Here," she scrambled out of the car, and ran towards him.

CHAPTER 7

There was no explanation that could get them out of trouble. The only thing to do was to tell the truth. No one came out of it well. It was after two o'clock before all the explanations were made, and Abby and Leo followed their father down the path from the Clarkes' house to their cottage. A stony-faced Mr Clarke watched them go. It was clear he hadn't finished dealing with the matter.

"We'll have to talk about this again in the morning," Dad said to Abby and Leo, after he'd thanked one of the other pickers who'd sat with Danny. "Apart from the deceit of the whole business, and the risks you took with your safety, there'll be the money side of things to sort out. There may be fines to pay. And if I were Ben Clarke, I probably wouldn't want to keep troublemakers working here."

But when morning came, there was no time to talk about anything. They'd slept in. Leo and Dad barely made it to work on time. Tony didn't make it to work at all. That was why someone else was driving the fork-lift when it crashed.

Abby heard Mr Clarke blame the new driver for the burst hydraulic hose that capsized the machine. Her father muttered something about the fork-lift being so old it should have been in a museum.

But what did it matter whose fault it was? No more crates could be carried until it was repaired. That was certain.

Abby knew Leo was in big trouble, but she had problems of her own, too. Mr Clarke was so angry he'd probably take back his permission for her and Danny to use the schoolroom. She could see her chance of finishing her plant story, and winning the computer, getting slimmer every minute. And Danny's butterfly eggs were still in the schoolroom. What a fuss there'd be if he couldn't get them back! He was doing such a good job of his pictures, too, with the help of Shelly's pens.

As there was no work, Leo had come home. Leaving Danny with him, Abby went to see what was happening. She watched Mr Clarke, bad-tempered from lack of sleep and worry about his daughter, storm back to the house to phone the mechanic. Keeping out of sight, Abby followed him, and waited behind a tree on the Clarkes' lawn. She hoped Shelly would come out of the house so she could catch up with her on any news.

"A hold-up like this would be bad at any time," she heard Ben Clarke tell his wife while he was waiting for someone to answer the phone. Mrs Clarke had just that minute arrived home from her trip, and was upstairs unpacking her bags.

"Yes, dear, but it won't take very long to fix," she said.

"Won't take long!" Ben Clarke shouted when he came away from the phone. "That fool of a mechanic fell off his roof this morning and broke his leg. He's in hospital!"

"But the relief mechanic will be on duty at this time of the year." Mrs Clarke's voice floated down from upstairs. "Get hold of her!"

"She's four hundred kilometres away at her son's wedding." Mr Clarke was beginning to roar. "We won't get the thing fixed before Tuesday!"

Through the window, Abby watched him pace up and down, with his hands jammed into his pockets and his face dark with worry.

"It can't be that bad," Mrs Clarke said, when she came downstairs.

"It couldn't be worse," he muttered. "The hot weather we've had since you've been away has ripened the fruit faster than we expected. If we can't pick until Tuesday, I hate to think how much we'll lose!"

"You were talking about buying a new fork-lift before this season started," Mrs Clarke reminded him.

"I know I was." He stopped, and glared at her. "But you insisted we get a new car!"

"Yes, dear. Well, perhaps I shouldn't have." She wasn't put out by his accusation, and just continued reasonably. "Isn't there one of the seasonal workers who'd know what to do? We've had mechanics here before."

Her husband shook his head. "No," he said. "Only Holloway, Leo and Abby's father. But after last night, I wouldn't trust any of them!" And he gave his wife a brief outline of what had happened.

Abby's cheeks burned with embarrassment, as she listened to the rather one-sided story.

"Anyway," he went on, "I'll go back and have a look at it myself."

Disappointed at not seeing Shelly, and not wanting to meet up with Mr Clarke, Abby scuttled through the trees beside the path, and back to the worried-looking crowd gathered around the damaged machine. A breakdown of any kind meant no work for anyone. And, since everyone was paid on contract, no work meant no money.

The fork-lift had capsized off the ramp leading into the shed. A crate was tipped upside down, and its load of oranges was scattered across the dirt track. It was more than a burst hydraulic hose. Even Abby could see that! And there was her father. He was reaching in among the greasy pipes and wires of the crippled machine.

"Just keep away from that!" roared Mr Clarke. The workers melted back as he charged up. "After last night, I don't want you interfering."

The talking stopped. Ben Clarke had always been a reasonable man. No one had ever heard him speak like that!

The silence lasted for three or four seconds, long enough for Dad to stand up and wipe his oily hands on a cloth. And long enough for Leo to lift Danny from his shoulders, where the child had been sitting to get a better view. Leo strode up to his angry employer, looked him straight in the eye, and said, "Nothing that happened last night was Dad's fault. But if you want your machine repaired, he's the only one to do it! No one knows more about those things than he does. But you'd better say please!" Leo turned around, took Danny's hand, and dragged him off through the crowd.

Mr Clarke opened his mouth, then closed it and scowled at Leo's back. "Well?" he demanded, turning and glaring at the group nearest to him. "What are you staring at?"

One of them murmured something to the others, and they all drifted off. Slowly, the rest of the onlookers followed until Abby was the only one left, half-hidden behind the packing shed door. She could see Dad and Mr Clarke standing there, facing each other.

"So, do you know anything about these machines?" Ben Clarke blustered. "Do you think you could fix it?"

"Probably," Dad replied. "If I had the parts."

"Oh, well, If you're going to try to get around me by pretending you know what you're doing, and then make excuses about not having any tools..."

"I didn't say that," Dad said in a low voice. "I may have all the necessary tools in my kit, but we'll also need a replacement hose and some other parts."

"I don't stock a spare parts shop. I leave that to the mechanic." Mr Clarke was speaking a little more calmly. "But maybe," he went on, "we could drive into town and get what we need."

"There's probably no need for that," Abby heard her father say. "You've got that old fork-lift in the other shed. We might be able to get what we want off that. It would save a bit of time and money."

After they'd disappeared, Abby went back to the cottage. She didn't know where Leo had gone, and someone had to make sure Danny didn't wander off. When she got there, Danny was by the door, intently watching his trapdoor spider drag a beetle into its tunnel. He was quite content.

It was Leo who needed watching. He lay face down on his bed, his arms wrapped around his pillow. Leo's shoulders shuddered as he tried to control his breathing.

"What's wrong?" Abby asked.

"Nothing." His voice was muffled.

"Do you always cry into your pillow?"

"Of course not!"

"What's wrong then?"

Leo lifted himself up on one elbow, and looked at his sister. His eyes were red-rimmed, and his lashes were wet.

"I've made a big mess of everything," he mumbled. "It was a stupid idea to take the car last night. I knew Tony was unreliable – but he promised..." He slumped back onto the bed. "I was just sick of hanging around here all the time. And Shelly really wanted to see that movie. She hardly gets to go anywhere."

While Leo was talking, Abby got to thinking about Shelly. She wondered what it would be like not to go to school and meet other kids. Shelly didn't even get away during the holidays. That was when her mum and dad were the busiest. Abby had been envious of all the things Shelly had, but maybe her life wasn't so special after all. Remembering how eager Shelly had been to make friends, and how she even enjoyed playing with a younger child like Danny, Abby realized how lonely Shelly must have been.

"And now I've ruined everything!" Leo had rolled over onto his back, and was staring at the ceiling. "I shouldn't have gone off at Mr Clarke like I did. I bet he'll fire me." He sat up and stared at Abby. "He might tell us all to go!" He stood up and strode across to the window. "But I couldn't help telling him off. He shouldn't have said those things to Dad."

"Hey, Abby," Jason's voice drifted in from outside. "Is Leo there?"

"What does he want?" muttered Leo, pulling back from the window. He didn't want to talk to any of the Bradfields. In fact, he didn't want to see anyone.

When Jason knocked a moment later, Abby opened the door. Leo was still hiding away in his bedroom.

"Hi, Abby." Jason flashed a friendly smile. "Is Leo here?"

"Why? Who wants him?" Abby asked.

"It's your dad. He said to get over to the shed. They need a hand."

"Who does?"

"Your dad and the boss. They think they can fix the fork-lift!"

CHAPTER 8

Just after nine o'clock, on her way to open the shop, Shelly dropped by to see Abby. "Aren't you going to the schoolroom this morning?"

"I didn't think your dad would want me to. Not after last night."

"Don't worry about that. Mum thinks it's a great idea, and she controls what goes on in there. Anyway, he still thinks you're perfect. Anyone who can clean up that mess in our kitchen has to be!" She laughed, and climbed back onto the four wheeler. "See you in a little bit," she called over her shoulder as she drove out onto the road.

Ten minutes later, Abby and Danny were on their way up to the schoolroom. Shelly had said it was all right, Abby kept reminding herself. All the same, her fingers still trembled as she turned the key in the schoolroom door. She couldn't forget Mr Clarke saying that he didn't trust any of the Holloways. Who on earth did he think he was, talking about their family like that?

The door swung open, and Danny rushed over to his jar of swan-plant cuttings. "Look!" he shouted. "Some of the eggs have hatched." He pointed to several tiny dark threads on the surface of the leaves.

The two of them crouched over the jar, their heads touching. Some leaves had little bites out of them. The baby caterpillars were eating! Leaving Danny still talking about the newly hatched caterpillars, Abby crept across to the computer. She had to record his words before she forgot them.

Soon she'd finished writing all she could about Danny and his caterpillars, and began working on her competition entry. As she typed away, she listened to Danny trying to count the tiny caterpillars over and over, still not certain how many there were.

"Six, I think," he muttered. "No, seven." Then Abby could hear his breathy voice counting again.

"Hard at work already?" A voice broke in on Abby's concentration. Her heart gave a couple of unexpected beats, and she swung around to see Mrs Clarke in the doorway, blocking out the morning sun.

"I hope it's all right for us to be here," Abby stammered. The woman's unexpected appearance had thrown her off balance.

"Of course it is. I'm glad to see the room get some use, especially during the holidays. Shelly only comes here when she has to."

Mrs Clarke walked across the room to stand at Abby's shoulder. "What are you writing?" she asked.

Abby could see where Shelly had got her blue eyes and friendly smile. She immediately felt comfortable explaining to Mrs Clarke about the story competition.

But when Mrs Clarke read the two pages Abby had already written, she said, "I see what you mean. It is difficult to write an interesting story about plants." Abby's confidence slumped. She'd been hoping her story wasn't as boring as she'd thought.

"Abby's writing a story about my butterflies," Danny interrupted.

"That's great!" replied Mrs Clarke, turning away from the computer and smiling at Danny. "And are you helping her?"

"No," said Danny. "I can't write. But Abby writes good stories," he went on proudly. "She's going to win a computer!" He pointed to the screen. "With that story."

But when Mrs Clarke, her smile fading, turned back to look at the screen, it was blank. "What did you do?" she asked.

"Erased it," mumbled Abby.

"Why?"

"Because it wasn't any good!" She looked up into Mrs Clarke's concerned face. "You knew it was awful, didn't you."

"Well," said Mrs Clarke, "you yourself said plants aren't very exciting to write about."

Abby stared down at her fingers, which twisted and turned in her lap.

Mrs Clarke put a soothing hand on Abby's shoulder. "Do you really have to enter that competition?" she asked.

"I don't have to," replied Abby, "if I don't want to win a computer."

"I see." The room was silent. Then Mrs Clarke suggested, "How about writing something else, just for a day or two? Write about something that's important to you."

"But what, though?" Abby asked. "Winning that competition is the most important thing to me right now."

"My butterflies are important," Danny interrupted, trying to help. His anxious eyes had watched Abby erase her story from the screen. "Don't erase them."

"Come and tell me about them," Mrs Clarke suggested, taking the child by the hand. "We'll leave Abby to do some thinking by herself." And they left her alone in the silent room.

Abby began by typing in the same old, horrible title. But no matter how hard she concentrated, she couldn't come up with even one good idea.

"Write about something that's important to you." She repeated Mrs Clarke's words. Remembering Danny saying that his butterflies were important, she pushed her chair back and went to look at them.

"Swan plants," she muttered. "Swan plants grow along the seashore around here. I'll write about Danny's swan plant."

An hour later, when Mrs Clarke and Danny returned with a jug of orange juice, three glasses, and some shortbread, Abby had written three pages of a story about the swan plant that grew on the hill near the beach.

"That's great," said Mrs Clarke, after she'd finished reading the printout that Abby had happily passed her.

"That story is about my swan plant, isn't it?" said Danny smugly. "And my butterflies are in it too, aren't they?"

"Yes," said Abby, looking at him curiously. Mrs Clarke hadn't read the story aloud. "How did you know?"

"It says 'butterfly' there." He jabbed one finger at the printout. "And there's 'swan plant'."

With a proud grin on his face, he pointed again. Then he said, "Bring my story up on screen, please. I want to read it on the computer."

As Abby loaded the disk with Danny's story on it, her fingers fumbled nervously. Danny had never before said that he wanted to read anything! She couldn't wait for the words to appear on the screen. When they did, there was only a second before Danny began.

"A monarch butterfly laid its eggs on a swan plant." The words came out slowly at first, then in a rush, he read, "Danny found them."

He looked up at Abby. "How was that?" he asked.

"Just great!" Abby hugged him. Danny pulled away and ran to the work table. "And here's the picture," he said. "Print the words out, please, and I can stick it on."

Abby could feel Danny's excitement, as he leaned on her chair and watched her print the page.

Shelly arrived in time to see the page, complete with text and picture, being pinned to the wall.

"There," said Mrs Clarke. "The first page of a wonderful story, written by Abby, and illustrated by Danny."

In between bites of shortbread, Danny insisted on rereading the page to Abby and Mrs Clarke, and then reading it twice to Shelly. When they'd finished eating, he demanded that Abby print out the next page, which was about putting the plant cutting in the peanut-butter jar. He had a picture for that, too.

It wasn't until they were packing up to go home for lunch, that Abby remembered again the ordeal of the previous night, and the panic about the smashed fork-lift. What if Dad couldn't fix it? It was ages since he'd done any of that sort of work. And the machine was so old. He might not find enough parts.

It was midday when they reached the cottage. Danny was hungry, but neither Dad nor Leo had come back. She hoped that was a good sign. They must still be working on the fork-lift.

Abby made some sandwiches. Danny ate his outside, watching over the trapdoor-spider's hole. Abby ate a small bite of hers, but she couldn't finish it.

While they'd been up at the schoolroom, all their worries had been forgotten in the excitement of Danny reading the butterfly story. And at last, Abby had managed to write something about plants that someone else might actually want to read.

But now, as they waited for Dad to come back, it seemed that everything depended on whether he was able to repair that machine.

What if he couldn't, and Mr Clarke told them to go before she could finish her story? Then she felt guilty. She was thinking only of herself.

Suddenly, a familiar roar split the silence.

"The fork-lift!" Danny yelled, and raced off towards the packing sheds. Abby chased after him. People tumbled out of bunk-houses and kitchens. They lined up along the edges of the road, as the fork-lift trundled out of the shed, a crate of oranges held high. Dad was driving, and Ben Clarke stood on the step beside him. Leo walked in front, his wide grin announcing their success.

The noisy machine stopped, and lowered its crate to the ground. Everyone cheered. They'd be working again after lunch. That meant money. Abby watched her father stop the engine and stand up on the seat. Grinning, he bowed to the cheering workers, then jumped to the ground. He and Ben Clarke turned to each other and shook hands that were black with grease.

CHAPTER 9

The school holidays ended that week. A woman came from town to look after the shop, while Shelly began spending most of her time studying in the schoolroom.

There were more barbecues on the Clarkes' lawn. Sometimes, Dad and Danny went, too. Dad and Mr Clarke spent hours discussing Dad's invention.

One evening, Mrs Clarke also invited Jason over for dinner. Mr Clarke frowned when Leo, Shelly, Jason, and Abby went to the dam afterwards for a swim. Abby heard Mrs Clarke tell him, "Don't be an old bear. Your little girl has to grow up sometime, you know."

The only shadow that dogged them was Leo's "driving without a licence" charge. Dad had helped him write a letter to the police about it, but there had been no reply.

At first, the end of the holidays didn't make much difference to Abby. She still prepared the meals, cleaned the cottage, and made sure Danny didn't get into too much trouble. On Mrs Clarke's invitation, she went to the schoolroom each day and used Shelly's computer for her writing. Finally, she completed her story for the competition, filled in the entry form, and put everything in the mailbox.

"Good luck," said Mrs Clarke. "I really like that story. I think it's got a good chance."

Abby managed a little smile, but she felt jittery inside.

With that job out of the way, she joined in with Shelly's school work, and went on with Danny's story.

At the end of the week, three of Danny's caterpillars had grown to an enormous size. One morning, he came into the schoolroom to find that one had become a chrysalis.

Abby sat at the computer and wrote, "The chrysalis hung upside down from the curtain rail. 'It looks like green glass,' Danny said."

On the following days, she added to the story. When she'd finished, she read it aloud to Danny. "Every day, Danny went to look at the chrysalis. On the fifth day, it was a darker green. Each day, it grew even darker. On the eighth day, it was almost black. The next morning, the chrysalis' skin split. Something crawled out. It looked like black, scrunched-up, wet paper.

"Danny was worried. 'That doesn't look like a butterfly,' he said.

"Danny didn't go home for lunch that day. He just sat and watched and waited.

"Then the sun came out and shone through the window. The butterfly sat in the sunshine and stretched its wings. It pumped them slowly up and down. It turned around on its spindly legs. Danny saw the orange-and-black wings.

"'Isn't it beautiful?' he said."

"That's the end," Abby said to Danny. "But I haven't got a title yet. What do you think we should name the story?"

"'The First Butterfly', of course," he said.

Abby was surprised at the way Danny had stuck at the job of finishing pictures for each page as it was printed, and even more surprised at how much he enjoyed reading it over and over.

That night, after dinner, they took Dad up to the schoolroom, and Danny read the story to him.

"I'm a good reader, aren't I, Dad?" Danny said, when he'd finished.

"You certainly are," Dad replied. "I've never heard you read so well!"

"I'll read it again if you like," suggested Danny. So, they stood there and listened to the story for the second time. "And now," he said to Abby, "will you please write me one called 'The Trapdoor's Tunnel'?"

That night, after she'd put Danny to bed, Abby wandered out into the living-room and sat on the couch. She was remembering how Danny hurried to get to the schoolroom each morning. He loved working on his pictures, and had begun writing as well. Sometimes, when Abby looked up from her own work, she could hear him chattering to Mrs Clarke out in the garden.

One day, when he wandered off, she found him in the kitchen making muffins with Mrs Clarke.

And that morning, he'd bought a bar of chocolate at the orchard shop. It was the kind that was wrapped in silver-and-purple paper. When they'd gone up to the schoolroom, he'd shoved it into Shelly's hands and said, "This is to make up for the chocolate I took."

"What should I do about it?" Shelly had asked Abby. "I don't want it. He can have it. It happened ages ago, and I knew he'd taken it."

"You have to keep it," Abby insisted. She tried to explain how this was the first time Danny had understood about stealing, and had tried to put it right.

It's because he loves it so much here, she thought.

It was Abby's stillness and silence that made Dad look up from the letter he was writing.

"Something wrong?" he asked, noticing her solemn expression.

Abby shook her head slowly. "Not wrong," she said, staring at the floor. "It just could be a little better."

"How do you mean?"

Abby shrugged.

"You've got something on your mind, haven't you?" Dad said. "You'd better tell me about it."

"Well," she began slowly. "You can see how much better Danny is, can't you?"

"His reading is better," Dad agreed.

"It's not only that," Abby insisted. "It's everything about him. He works really hard at anything Mrs Clarke gets him to do. He wrote a story all by himself this morning. And he finished a whole page of Shelly's old maths book."

"That's great," agreed Dad. "Maybe by the time we go home, he'll be able to work well by himself."

"If we go home, I reckon he'll just slip back." Abby's fingers twisted together.

"You want to stay out in the country?" Dad said, suddenly realizing what she was getting at.

"Can't we?" she begged.

"No." He shook his head. "The season will be over soon, and there'll be no work. Besides, where would we live?"

"We could stay here at the cottage," she begged. "And you and Mr Clarke are friends now. He would give you a job."

"I thought you hated this cottage. Last month, you said you couldn't wait to go home."

"But I like it now."

"You wouldn't like it when the winter comes. It gets so cold!"

"It can't get that bad. Shelly lives here in the wintertime. She wouldn't like it if it was as cold as all that."

Dad frowned, and stared at her for a minute. Then he said, "Is it Jason?" Abby shook her head, but she kept her eyes on the floor. "Then it's that computer, and all the other things in Shelly's schoolroom, isn't it?"

"It's everything," Abby agreed. "I couldn't have written my story for the competition without the computer. But it's Danny, too." And she told him how worried she was about Danny going to school on his own when they got home.

Dad pushed his chair back, and came to sit beside her. "Look, Abby, I know you've enjoyed it here, but it's simply not practical to consider staying. There'll be no more work after the end of next week."

"As soon as that?"

Where had the last few weeks gone?

Dad nodded. "In fact, we should leave earlier. This letter," he tapped one finger on the sheet of paper, "is about an interview for a job."

"But you didn't say anything about getting a job after we leave here!"

Everything was beginning to pile up on Abby all at once.

"I didn't want to tell you until I was sure. We've had a lot of disappointments this year. This might have been another one."

"Then you aren't certain about the work?" Abby couldn't believe she'd even asked that question, and her cheeks flamed red. Her selfishness made her feel guilty.

"It's with my old firm. A new manager has taken over. He says they should never have laid me off in the first place. The interview is just a formality. The job's mine if I want it."

"That's great," Abby said, bowing her head in an attempt to hide her disappointment.

"Look, Abby," Dad said gently, taking her hand. "If you're worrying about Danny and how he's going to get by without you next year, I think you'd better stop. It's time he learned to look after himself. You've been wonderful to him, but even real mothers have to know when to let their children stand on their own feet."

Abby tried to swallow the lump that came up in her throat. She blinked to clear the tears blurring her eyes. "I know, but..." No more words would come.

"And then there's you," Dad went on. "You don't spend enough time on yourself. Danny will take advantage of you if you let him. You know that, don't you?"

"Yes," Abby whispered. She had to agree. But in wanting to stay here, she *was* thinking of herself. She'd never found it so easy to write. In addition, by working with Shelly, she'd sorted out a lot of problems she used to have with maths and other subjects. It was also much easier to cook meals and look after everyone when school was only two minutes away. And then there was Jason.

"There's one other thing," Dad said. "Mrs Clarke has been very kind allowing you and Danny to use Shelly's schoolroom, but you can't expect that to go on forever." He hesitated. Then he said, "Maybe Shelly could come and stay with us during the holidays."

Abby didn't answer, but at that moment, she realized that missing Shelly wasn't the problem. They didn't have that much in common. They'd never be really great friends. Not the kind of friends who'd keep in touch from a distance. The only reason they got along well together now was that there was really no one else to hang out with, Abby thought to herself.

She couldn't sleep that night. She turned to face the wall, trying to block out the moonlight that shone through the skimpy curtains, but it didn't help. Although she wanted to keep her mind on the good things that had happened, such as swimming at the Clarkes' dam and Danny starting to read, the prospect of leaving the orchard kept nagging at her.

Another thing that kept her awake was knowing that the story competition results would be out any day. That should have been something to look forward to. Mrs Clarke's encouragement had made Abby feel she had a good chance of winning. Going home wouldn't be so bad if a computer was waiting for her when she got there. But, what would she do if she didn't win?

Early the next morning, Abby hurried up the path to the schoolroom. Danny had to run to keep up with her. "Wait for me," he panted. "What's the hurry?"

Abby wasn't looking forward to explaining how they had to go home soon. How there wasn't much time. Danny would be upset. To put off telling him, she said, "I want to finish your trapdoor-spider story this morning." That was true. She had to get it finished before they left. And while she was writing, she might forget about having to leave.

Just before lunch-time, Abby printed out the last page, and Danny stuck on the picture.

Mrs Clarke pinned it on the wall. "That's an even better story than the one about the butterfly," she said, standing back and gazing at the story.

"I can read this story, too," announced Danny, and he did, twice.

"You must be one of the best readers I know," Mrs Clarke said, giving him a hug. "But now you've got to go home. You don't want your dad coming back and finding no lunch, do you?"

Danny shook his head. He pulled away from Mrs Clarke and bounded out the door. "Come on, Abby," he called.

Abby turned off the computer, stood up slowly, and ambled across to the door, where Mrs Clarke was waiting to lock up. "We've only got a few more days here," Abby blurted out. She was appalled to find she was crying. With both hands clenched at her sides, she turned her head, attempting to hide her tears.

"Never mind," Mrs Clarke said, trying to console her. "We've had a wonderful summer together. I know Shelly has just loved having you here, but even she knows it can't go on forever."

Instead of helping Abby control her tears, Mrs Clarke's kindness brought them on in a great flood.

"Now then," Mrs Clarke murmured. She put both arms around the sobbing girl, gently rocking her from side to side. "This isn't the end of the world. When you get home, it will be like you've never been away. And what about that competition you're going to win? The results should be out any day now." She sat Abby on the nearest chair, and gave her a handkerchief.

Between sobs, Abby explained her worries about Danny coping at school by himself. She tried to express how much she was going to miss the orchard classroom and the independence of being able to work on her own, but she couldn't find the words.

"It's great at first," Mrs Clarke said, guessing the truth behind Abby's stammering, "but it can be very lonely. You ask Shelly."

"Ask me what?" Shelly said. She bounded up the steps with a bundle of envelopes in her hand, and stood in the doorway sorting through them. Not waiting for an answer, she exclaimed,

"There's one here for you, Abby. I bet it says you've won the competition!" She thrust the envelope into Abby's trembling hands.

Dropping the screwed-up handkerchief on the floor, Abby ripped at the envelope. Her heart thumped, and she couldn't breathe. It was ages before her trembling fingers pulled out a folded piece of paper, and flattened it out on her lap. Her eyes scanned the page, searching for her name – but it wasn't there!

She hadn't won the competition. Vicky Raymond had. In spite of beating Vicky last year, Abby hadn't even been placed!

CHAPTER 10

From the moment Abby discovered she hadn't won the competition, everything seemed to happen. Leo got a letter telling him that, considering the circumstances, the police didn't intend to prosecute him for driving without a licence. And Dad got a letter, in the same delivery, cancelling his interview. The manager said that the interview was only a formality, and it would be fine for him to start back at work on the following Monday. That gave them only two days to pack up, clean the cottage, and drive back to the city. It was just as well. It gave Abby no time to brood on her failure.

"Did you remember my books?" Danny asked as Abby filled a cardboard box with the last-minute things that wouldn't fit in the bags.

He'd unpinned the pages from the schoolroom wall that morning, and Mrs Clarke had helped him staple them together. Abby nodded. She'd hardly spoken since the rotten competition results had arrived. No one had noticed her silence. They'd all been much too excited about going home.

It was early Sunday afternoon, and at last everything was piled into the car, and the goodbyes had been said. Abby looked out the back window as the car rumbled through the orchard gates, and waved to Shelly. The last thing she saw was the yellow sun shining on her friend's blonde hair. There was no sign of Jason. She hadn't seen him since Friday, when she'd told him they were going to be leaving. Leo said he hadn't seen him, either.

Abby reached one arm behind Danny to console herself by giving him a hug. At least he still needed her. But the boy's thin shoulders impatiently wriggled free.

"I'll be going to school on my own tomorrow, Abby!" he said. Abby stared at him.

He wanted to go by himself! He didn't need her to look after him any more.

"And I'm taking my books to school. I'm going to read them to Miss Deane. She'll get a big surprise, won't she!" He bounced up and down on the seat.

"What about James Raymond?" said Abby. "What if...?" Then she stopped. I'm trying to scare him, she thought.

"I don't care about James!" Danny boasted, bouncing a few more times. "He won't be able to read my books."

Abby turned her face to the window. She didn't want him to see her tears. It looked like Dad was right. Danny would be able to get by just fine without her.

The next morning, Abby dressed in the new clothes she and Dad had bought before the holidays.

"You look very nice," Dad said. "It's a good thing we bought those before we went away."

After breakfast, Abby sent an excited Danny out the door on his own. Clutching his precious books under one arm, Danny ran down the driveway without looking back. Abby tried to ignore the lurch her heart gave. She put on her jacket and set off across town on her bike.

When she arrived at school, she went straight to the office, where the secretary, a round-faced, smiling woman, gave her a slip of paper with her name and room number written on it.

"Down that corridor, dear," she said, pointing. "The third door on the left."

As she waited for the teacher to find her a seat, Abby was pleased to see some girls from her old school – but not Vicky, she thought with relief. They waved and smiled, pleased to see her. Either they didn't know, or they didn't care, about the results of the story competition. She hoped they didn't remember how she'd crowed about winning last year.

The first half of the morning went by in a whirl. Abby needed to catch up with all the things everyone else had already had a month to get used to. She had no time to worry about how Danny was getting along.

Then, during morning break, she heard a small group talking in the corner of the hallway. It was Vicky Raymond and her group of friends. Abby hadn't seen them all summer.

"And the prize was a computer!" Vicky was saying. "I don't know what I'll do with it. I've already got a computer." The others giggled, and huddled close.

"I'm glad you beat Abby Holloway," one of the others said. "What place did she get?"

"I don't think she was placed," Vicky replied, her eyes flicking sideways to make sure Abby was listening. Then they all giggled some more.

They'd ruined Abby's day almost before it had started. She couldn't concentrate on anything, and was glad when the bell rang to go home. It was only then that she remembered Danny. Without saying goodbye, she left her friends in the crowded corridor and pushed her way outside. She grabbed her bike and pedalled for home.

As she biked across town, Abby grew more and more anxious. Danny had never come home to an empty house. What would he do when he realized she wasn't there?

As she turned the last corner, her anxiety had turned to panic. She pictured Danny in the kitchen, trying to make himself a hot drink. He might burn himself on the boiling water!

But, as she skidded to a stop at the gate and hurried up the path, there was no sound of crying. There was no sound at all! She dropped her bike and went inside, but the house was empty. Where was he?

Abby ran outside. Surely he couldn't have got lost on the way home. The school was only in the next block.

Then, as she stared up and down the block, she heard voices laughing and shouting from further up the street.

"My turn now," yelled one voice.

"That's Danny," Abby muttered. She followed the noise as far as the house with the white fence – Vicky Raymond's house. There was a basketball hoop fastened to the side of the garage. Danny and James were struggling underneath it for possession of the ball. Abby opened her mouth to shout at James to give the ball to Danny. Then she saw Danny's wide grin. He wasn't upset. He was getting by just fine on his own.

Abby turned away. She wasn't sure whether she was relieved that Danny was all right, or disappointed because he was doing so well at looking after himself. But disappointment was winning as she stopped at their letter-box to collect the mail.

Abby had hardly started going through the pile of letters when the phone rang.

"Abby?" It was Shelly Clarke.

For a moment, Abby forgot about Danny. What could Shelly want?

"I just called to say hello," Shelly said. Abby didn't believe that even Shelly would make a long-distance call just for that, and she could hear her bubbling laughter. She was excited about something. Then Shelly went on, "It's Mum who really wants to talk to you. She's got some news for you."

"Give me that phone, Shelly," Abby heard Mrs Clarke say in the background. Then she said, "Is that you, Abby?"

"Yes," Abby answered. Remembering her manners, she added, "How are you, Mrs Clarke?"

"Fine, thank you, Abby." She hesitated for a second. What does she want? Abby wondered to herself.

Then Mrs Clarke went on. "It's about the stories you wrote."

"But I didn't come anywhere with them in the competition," interrupted Abby.

"I know," said Mrs Clarke. "I was there when you got the results, remember? I'm talking about the butterfly story, and the other one about the spider."

"Danny brought them back home with him," Abby reminded her.

"But they are still on the computer..."

So what? thought Abby.

"And when the sales representative for the Books for Kids publishing company was here, just after you finished the first one, I showed it to him. I hope you don't mind."

"Of course not." Abby liked people to read her stories.

"He took a copy of it to show his editor. I didn't want to say anything just then, in case nothing came of it, but she liked it, and she called and asked for your home address. I told her about your spider story, and she wants to see that, too! She's sending you a contract. It might be there by now!"

A contract. Abby had heard about contracts from a writer who came to speak during Book Week at school. A contract meant her story would be published!

Abby dropped the phone. She ignored the distant sound of Mrs Clarke's voice, and rummaged through the mail until she came up with a large brown envelope addressed to Miss Abby Holloway. Across the top was the Books for Kids logo.

Abby could hardly breathe as she slid her thumb under the flap of the envelope and pulled out a letter.

"Dear Miss Holloway," she read, "We would like to include your story *The First Butterfly* in our series of science books written by teenagers for younger readers. Two copies of our contract are included. If you agree with our conditions, please sign both copies and return them to us.

"We would also be interested in seeing another story that we understand you've written, titled *The Trapdoor's Tunnel*."

Slowly, Abby put the letter down and picked up the phone. "Mrs Clarke, are you still there?"

"Yes, I'm here. What happened?"

"Books for Kids wants to publish my butterfly story." Abby's voice was hardly more than a whisper, as though she could scarcely believe what she was saying.

"I thought they might."

"And would you please make a copy of my spider story and send it to them?"

"Yes, of course I'll do that, Abby. And congratulations. That's wonderful news!"

"Yes. Thank you. Goodbye." Abby put down the phone and picked up the letter. She was halfway through reading it for the second time when Leo flung the front door open and headed for the kitchen.

"Look at this," she said as he came away from the bench, biting into a thick peanut-butter sandwich. She handed him the letter. He read it and looked up at her with startled eyes.

"Where's this contract they're talking about?" he asked.

Abby gave it to him. His eyes scanned the pages as he chewed his sandwich.

"Have you read this?" he asked after he'd finished reading. She shook her head.

"Not yet."

"Well, you'd better! They're going to pay you a lot of money, just for one story. And if they like it, they'll publish the other one, too – the one about the spider."

"Let me see," Abby grabbed the papers from his hand.

Leo was right. Five hundred dollars up front for one story! And possibly more later on, depending on sales. She would have been happy just to see them in print!

"What are you going to do with all that money, Abby?" demanded Leo. "Take us all out shopping?"

"I don't think so!" grinned Abby, and she pulled an advertisement for computers out of the pile of letters. She waved it around before slapping it down on the table.

Then she opened another letter she'd found in the bundle of mail. It was addressed to her, and the sender's name was on the back of the envelope – Jason Bradfield.

It looked as if things were going to be OK this year, after all!

FROM THE AUTHOR

The characters in *Who Will Look Out for Danny?* are a mixture of several children I've known.

First of all, there's Danny. He's one of those children who has difficulty learning to read. Then, one day, something turns on the light, in just the way Danny's creepy-crawlies do for him.

Then there's Abby, who worries about Danny so much, she has a hard time getting on with her own life. Abby is quite envious of Shelly – that is, until she sees that Shelly's life is not as wonderful as she thought.

Leo is friendly and fun, but he thinks only about himself. He doesn't realize how important his family is to him until, one day, he almost brings disaster on everyone.

I put the three children and their father into one family, sent them off fruit picking, and waited to see what they would do. The result is *Who Will Look Out for Danny?*

MARIE GIBSON

FROM THE ILLUSTRATOR

I really enjoyed the challenge of illustrating
Who Will Look Out for Danny? I found the story to
be very uplifting. It stirred deep, fond memories of
my own childhood, when my family and I spent our
summer holidays travelling around New Zealand,
camping and picking fruit.

I was also inspired by
the compassion and
willingness of some of the
characters to support and
encourage each other. I
think this willingness to
help out is very important
and should be encouraged
in our communities.

I particularly liked the happy ending in *Who Will
Look Out for Danny*? Everything worked out well for
all of the characters.

KELVIN HAWLEY

Who Will Look Out for Danny?

ISBN 13: 978-0-79-011685-3
ISBN 10: 0-79-011685-5

 Kingscourt

Published by:
McGraw-Hill Education
Shoppenhangers Road, Maidenhead, Berkshire, England, SL6 2QL
Telephone: 44 (0) 1628 502730
Fax: 44 (0) 1628 635895
Website: www.kingscourt.co.uk
Website: www.mcgraw-hill.co.uk

Written by **Marie Gibson**
Illustrated by **Kelvin Hawley**
Edited by **Frances Bacon**
Designed by **Nicola Evans**

Original Edition © 1997 Shortland Publications
English Reprint Edition © 2010 McGraw-Hill Publishing Company

Printed in Hong Kong through Colorcraft Ltd